W0334767

NOUVELLE STAR IN
HOLLYWOOD
ALEX'S JOURNAL

Tip Tongue JOURNAL

À lire progressivement en anglais !

Tip Tongue Journal, c'est un carnet de voyage linguistique palpitant

Les héros, jeunes Français comme le lecteur, racontent et dessinent leurs aventures avec des amis anglophones dans un journal de bord, qu'ils s'efforcent de rédiger progressivement dans la langue de Shakespeare (le dernier chapitre est à 100% en anglais).

Avec Tip Tongue Journal, lire et écrire de l'anglais devient naturel

Pas besoin de dictionnaire, les héros font tout le boulot. Un plaisir de lecture immense, la fierté de comprendre une langue étrangère, et une incitation à écrire, se raconter, dessiner, comme le font les personnages, et ainsi mémoriser plus et mieux.

Avec Tip Tongue Journal, on découvre les vertus du crayon et du stylo !

Dans leur journal, les héros prennent leurs crayons et leurs stylos pour explorer la langue et la mémoriser à leur manière. Ils utilisent sans le savoir des méthodes de mémorisation et de créativité : *sketchnoting, doodle, bullet journal*... C'est amusant, et efficace !

L'audio-book

Tout comme dans la collection de romans **Tip Tongue**, chaque titre offre une version intégrale audio téléchargeable. Un véritable bain de langue pour découvrir comment se prononce un mot en langue étrangère au moment où on le lit.

Pour découvrir la collection, accéder aux audio-books et aux ressources pédagogiques :

https://tip-tongue-anglais.syros.fr/
Ou téléchargez l'appli **Syros Live** et flashez les couvertures.

La collection des romans Tip Tongue se décline en anglais, espagnol, allemand, et pour tous les âges de 8 à 16 ans et plus !

Elle a obtenu en 2015 le **Label européen des langues**, récompensant l'excellence en matière d'apprentissage innovant. Chaque titre correspond à un niveau cible du CECRL (Cadre européen commun de référence pour les langues), sur lequel sont basés les programmes scolaires.

Pour choisir son Tip Tongue

- 1 / 8-10 ans / CE2-CM1-CM2 / A1 Introductif
- 2 / 10-12 ans / CM2-6e-5e / A1 Découverte
- 3 / 12-14 ans / 5e-4e-3e / A2 Intermédiaire
- 4 / 14-16+ ans / 3e-2nde-1re / B1 Seuil

**TIP TONGUE, C'EST TOUT UN PROGRAMME :
PLAISIR, CURIOSITÉ, CONFIANCE EN SOI, RÉUSSITE !**

Tip Tongue JOURNAL

Une collection dirigée par Stéphanie Benson

Label européen des langues

ISBN : 978-2-74-852494-9

25, avenue Pierre-de-Coubertin, 75013 Paris
Loi n° 49-956 du 16 juillet 1949
sur les publications destinées à la jeunesse,
modifiée par la loi n° 2011-525 du 17 mai 2011.

N°éditeur: 10237783 - Dépôt légal: février 2019

NOUVELLE STAR IN HOLLYWOOD

ALEX'S JOURNAL

Stéphanie Benson

Illustrations de Juliette Maroni

SYROS

Bon, j'ai promis à ma prof d'anglais d'écrire un journal, c'est elle qui m'a offert ce cahier ! Hello, Mrs Jones! Alors autant commencer tout de suite. Sans compter qu'il n'y a pas grand-chose d'autre à faire ici. I am on a plane to Los Angeles (a flight of 12 hours).

SO... JOURNAL, LET'S GO !

OUTILS NÉCESSAIRES :

1. la date en anglais, ☑
2. la météo, ☑
3. les sentiments, ☑
4. ce que je fais. ☑

In English: 1) The Date, 2) The Weather, 3) Feelings, 4) What I do.

THIS JOURNAL
EST LA PROPRIÉTÉ DE
APPARTIENT À

is the property of

belongs to

Surname:
Giordano

First name:
Alexandre

Nationality:
French

Address:
Appartement 109,
21 rue du Grenier
Saint-Lazare, 75001,
PARIS, France

attention, 2 «d» dans «adresse» en anglais

Date of birth:
15th January

Age:
14 years old
(I AM fourteen)
like I AM hungry,
I AM cold, et pas I have,
comme en français

Eyes:
Brown

Hair:
Brown

Favourite place:
NEW YORK
(Where I met Diandra)*

*cf. *Alex et le rêve de la New York Star*, collection « Tip Tongue ».

MONDAY 3RD JANUARY

Voilà pour la date. La météo, je sais pas. What's the weather like on a plane?

I'M ON A PLANE... ET ON PLANE AU-DESSUS DES NUAGES.

Donc, je suis dans l'avion (ON the plane et pas IN comme en français) en direction de (going to).

HOLLYWOOD !!!

↳ *Énorme, non ?*

I feel happy, excited, WOW!
Because, as I said:

I'M GOING TO HOLLYWOOD !!!

I'm going to Hollywood, near Los Angeles, because Diandra* m'a invité. Because Diandra invited me!!! Ça paraît dingue quand on y pense, mais le fait est que je suis devenu ami avec une star du rap mondialement connue (enfin, surtout aux USA, mais c'est déjà pas mal).

ONE THING ABOUT AMERICAN CULTURE

AMERICANS LIKE RAP MUSIC

AMERICANS INVENTED RAP MUSIC

Et c'est ma copine. Pas copine copine, juste une « friend ». Comme une « best friend ». On s'est rencontrés cet été à New York à un moment où elle tentait d'échapper à la pression du star-system, et on est devenus amis. Sur son prochain album, il y a un titre dont le refrain est en français et elle veut avoir un « perfect accent ». J'ai promis que j'allais l'aider.

The new Star of Rap, Diandra is amazing!

*Diandra is an American rap star and she's really famous in the USA.

HER EMAIL

Hi Alex!
How are you? Good, I hope. Listen, on my next album*, there's a song with a chorus in French. Would you please come and coach me so I have a perfect accent? All expenses paid, of course. It's in Hollywood coz I'll be recording the video clip at the same time. Please say yes! Your One and Only Super American Friend, Diandra.

*J'ai souligné les mots-clefs

À la première lecture, j'ai en gros saisi. Je n'en croyais pas mes yeux. J'ai relu 3 fois, puis j'ai appelé ma mère pour confirmation.
Le refrain en français est un mince prétexte, mais une star obtient tout ce qu'elle veut, non ? Et Diandra ME veut avec elle à Hollywood !!!

Sur son prochain album, il y a une chanson avec un refrain en français, elle te demande de la coacher, et ça se passera à Hollywood parce qu'elle tourne le clip vidéo en même temps...

Maman

Maman hésite, se rend compte de ce qu'elle vient de lire.

Mais c'est sérieux ???
Elle t'invite à Hollywood ???

Maman
(voix un peu aiguë)

Ben... je crois, oui.

Moi

Mais ça va prendre combien de temps ? Tu permets que je lui pose quelques questions ?

Maman

Ce dialogue a été suivi d'un échange par mail entre maman et Diandra :

(c'est moi qui tape)

MAMAN	DIANDRA
How long will Alex stay in Hollywood?	Six or seven weeks
What about school?	There's a school here essentially for movie kids
Who will the adults be?	My parents, my manager, staff, teachers
How much will it cost?	Nothing for you. We'll pay for everything. Even the taxi to the airport
Are you sure?	Yes! I'm a rap star!!
Can we think about it?	Sure, take your time
When do you need an answer?	Tomorrow :-)

L'hôtesse de l'air vient distribuer des pancakes. Je ne sais plus si c'est le petit déjeuner ou le dessert du soir ! J'ai démarré ce journal en transcrivant les mails et dialogues. Ma prof d'anglais m'a convaincu qu'ainsi mes progrès seraient fulgurants !

J'ai entouré les questions pour m'en souvenir.

HOW LONG? ⇨ **Combien de temps ?** (How = Comment, like How are you? Comment vas-tu ?)

HOW MUCH? ⇨ **Combien** ça pèse, coûte, en fonction de la suite de la phrase.

WHAT ABOUT? ⇨ **Et en ce qui concerne ?** (Chanson de Michael Jackson, *Earth Song*, *What about us*)

WHO? ⇨ **Qui ?** Facile.

WHEN? ⇨ **Quand ?** Today, tomorrow, yesterday, the day after yesterday, before tomorrow (Today, Monday January 3rd)

ARE YOU SURE? ⇨ Yes I am sure.

CAN WE THINK? ⇨ Yes we can (campagne d'élection de Barack Obama, PRES USA)

THEN... Mum asked Dad, Dad said OK, Mum said OK, Mum asked me, I said **YES!!!**

Attendez, on annonce quelque chose... Beginning our approach to... fasten your seat-belts... Ça y est, on arrive!!! HOLLYWOOD!!!

TUESDAY 4TH JANUARY

Twelve hours ON a plane is LONG...

MAIS À L'ARRIVÉE À

L.A.

Los Angeles

J'AI ÉTÉ ACCUEILLI COMME UN

V.I.P.

Very Important Person IN ENGLISH.

avec

UN VÉRITABLE « *Welcome Committee* ».

Press Agent, Security Guard,
Personal Assistant, Chauffeur...
and... Diandra!

J'ai des papillons dans le ventre.

ELLE N'A PAS CHANGÉ, QUELLE ÉMOTION !!!

Hi Alex!
Good to see you.
Have a good flight?

Voici Diandra, who I met the first time in New York. Devant tout ce monde, on est un peu coincés tous les deux... Notre rencontre avait été si intense !

Yes, great, thanks!
How are you?

I'm good. Shall we go?
The hotel's not far...

Hotel... Je vais vivre dans un hôtel... ??
Pendant 5 ou 6 semaines??

LUXURY!

Et quand je dis luxury... C'est comme au cinéma ! I'm in Hollywood! I'm dreaming! Ma ‹‹ chambre ›› (room) est composée d'une chambre avec un lit énorme, d'une salle de bains avec baignoire à bulles, d'un salon avec bar cuisine et une immense télé, et d'un dressing...

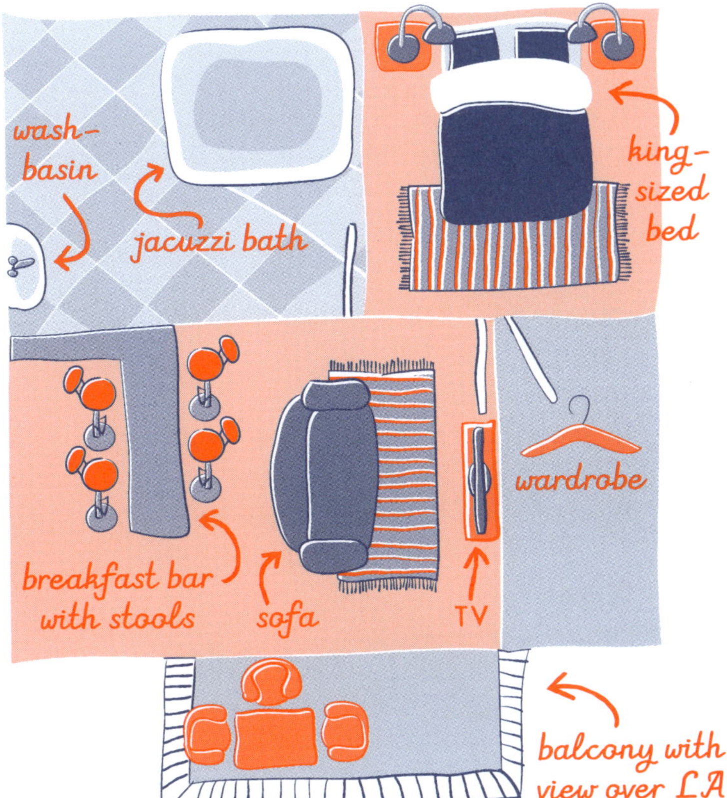

MY ROOM IN THE PLAZZA HOTEL L.A.

Diandra m'a laissé du temps pour défaire mes valises (to unpack) et trouver mes marques (settle in), et a posé sur le bar de la cuisine (breakfast bar) mon emploi du temps :

ALEX'S SCHEDULE

TUESDAY

7pm Dinner.
(Mexican, hope you like Mexican food)

WEDNESDAY

9 am School.
-> (see separate timetable for lessons)
12 pm Lunch at school.
-> (it's usually not too bad)
2 pm Rehearsals in recording studio with me.
-> (singing)
5 pm Rehearsals in film studio with me.
-> (dancing)
7 pm Dinner.
-> hamburger joint downtown L.A.

Yes, I need to rehearse!

Répétitions

SO NOW: DINNER!

Yes! I love Mexican food.

se prononce

WEDNES(WENZ)DAY JANUARY 5TH

Le restau d'hier était fantastique... Même si je n'ai pas compris grand-chose et je n'ai pas ouvert la bouche ! Une dame m'a apporté le petit déj' dans ma chambre ! Et mon emploi du temps. J'y crois pas !

ONLY THREE HOURS OF SCHOOL!

SCHOOL DAY 1

9 am > 10 am English
10 am > 11 am English
11 am > 12 am English
12 am > LUNCH

Very varied timetable!

On est dix dans la classe. On m'a mis à côté d'une brune aux yeux bleus qui s'appelle Lily Jessop.

Diandra, ayant deux ans de plus, n'est pas avec nous... dommage...

CONVERSATION WITH LILY

Lily

Hey, Alex! My name's Lily! Diandra's my friend. She's told me all about you. She said you'd be here today. She's sooooo talented, isn't she? I mean I'm sooooo pleased to actually meet someone from France. You know, real France! I mean like in the movies! I mean, wow! What's it like, France, you know? Are all the French guys sexy like you with that crazy accent?

Me

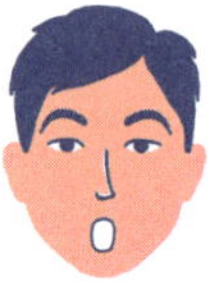

Euh... (en pensant : c'est la première fois qu'une fille me trouve sexy, ok, je suis pas mal, mais quand même. Et comment peut-elle me parler de mon accent ??? J'ai pas encore pu en placer une !)

Lily m'a pris sous son aile. Elle m'a aidé à comprendre ce que disait la prof grâce à des petits dessins. On a étudié un poème d'Emily Dickinson, une Américaine qui a vécu au 19e siècle.

LE VOILÀ
(avec les dessins de Lily) :

She sights a Bird — she chuckles —

She flattens — then she crawls —

She runs without the look of feet —

Her eyes increase to Balls —

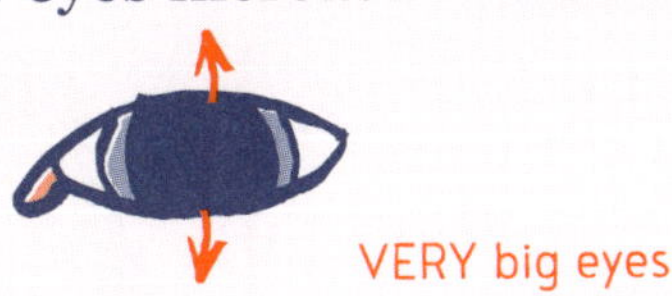

En gros, elle voit un oiseau, elle rigole. Elle s'aplatit puis rampe. Elle court sans qu'on voie ses pattes. Ses yeux s'agrandissent comme des balles. Ça ressemble assez à mon chat !

Lily helped me understand the poem.

LILY IS NICE

Lily is just so wonderful! She's pretty, she's fun and just... I don't know... so NICE

Diandra

(description of Lily by Diandra)

Diandra is just so amazing! She's beautiful and talented and such a good singer, and wow! can she dance!

(description of Diandra by Lily)

Lily

Lily and Diandra are friends. Lily's dad is the film director for Diandra's clip (Lloyd Jessop).

LUNCH WITH DIANDRA AND LILY

Tacos and salad*

The weather is sunny and warm.

Lily and Diandra are talking... et je ne comprends rien. Ça va trop vite. De temps à autre je saisis un mot ou deux. Voilà ce que j'ai compris :

JUST VOCALS

DANCE ROUTINE

TOO EXPENSIVE

I SO LOVE MEXICAN FOOD

NO MUSICIANS

FRENCH

* Ce sont des galettes de blés (tortillas) avec des trucs dessus genre bœuf bourguignon ou poulet basquaise.

C'est fou ! Je suis assis dans la cantine (canteen) d'une école super chic de Los Angeles en compagnie des deux filles les plus belles de la planète ! Puisque je ne comprends rien à leur conversation, je les dessine.

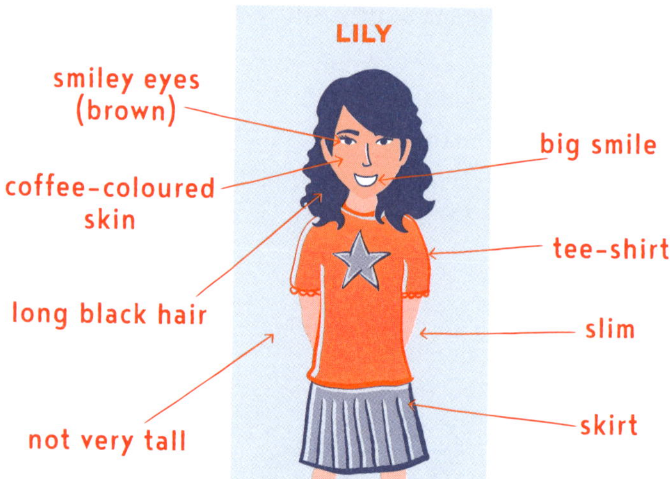

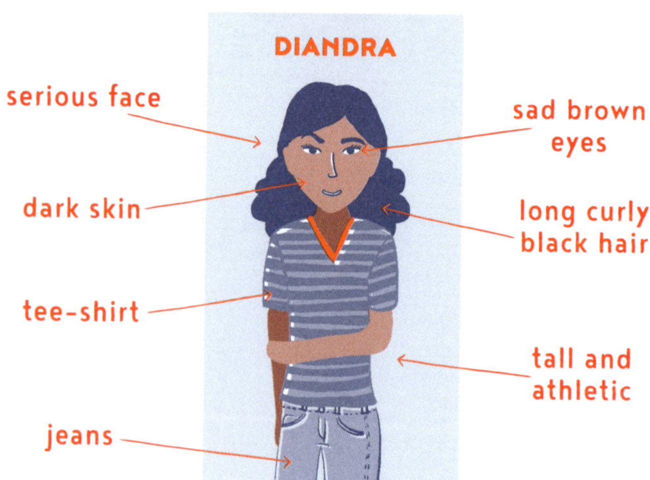

LATER IN MY HOTEL ROOM

Je viens de passer l'après-midi le plus génial de ma vie !

(Lily told me what to write in English)

THE BEST AFTERNOON OF MY LIFE

FIRST = Music Studio, Diandra sings, Lily and I listen, I tell her the French pronunciation, we laugh (ha! ha! ha!)

Prononcer : laffe

SECOND = Dance Studio, Diandra dances, Lily and I watch, Diandra's dancing teacher is really strict (Lily doesn't like him).

Et maintenant, en attendant le restaurant du soir, j'ai des devoirs.

YES! HOMEWORK.

Write a portrait of yourself in poetry like Emily Dickinson

short descriptions with hyphens (tirets)

This is my homework

I'm brown – with dark eyes –
I'm a French boy –
In New York –
I met a star.

Today I've eaten lunch in L. A. –
Paris is very far.

Bon, d'accord, c'est pas exactement un portrait, mais c'est ce que je ressens. Tout d'un coup, Paris semble loin.

FAR, FAR AWAY...

THURSDAY 6TH JANUARY

The weather is beautiful. It's sunny!

Today I have 3 hours at school. Three hours of American History about the **STATE OF CALIFORNIA**. Je n'ai pas compris grand-chose. Mais j'ai recopié les mots-clefs que le prof écrivait sur le tableau :

MOST POPULATED STATE IN USA

THIRD BIGGEST STATE IN USA

BIGGEST ECONOMY IN THE USA

THE ORIGIN OF THE FILM INDUSTRY

FREE STATE = AGAINST SLAVERY

NEXT WEEK'S SCHEDULE

Et j'ai eu mon emploi du temps de la semaine prochaine.

MONDAY	**3 hours Math**
TUESDAY	**3 hours Science**
WEDNESDAY	**3 hours English**
THURSDAY	**3 hours History**
FRIDAY	**3 hours Science**

J'ai compris. Une matière par jour, seulement le matin. L'après-midi est consacré aux répétitions ou aux cours privés.

Tomorrow afternoon, Lily has tennis lessons.

Ce soir, j'ai fait un peu mieux la connaissance des parents de Diandra et de ceux de Lily. Les parents de Diandra sont cool.
Diandra's parents are really cool. Her Mom has really dark skin, her Dad is more coffee-coloured.
(Je remarque donc que, côté couleur de peau, Diandra est proche de son père.)

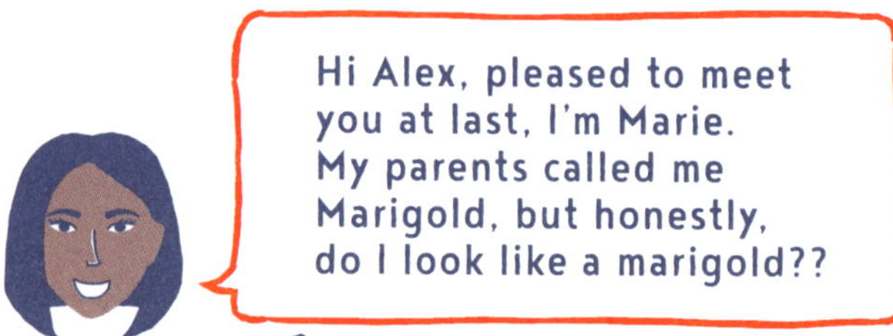

(marigold, c'est un œillet d'Inde, une fleur orange)

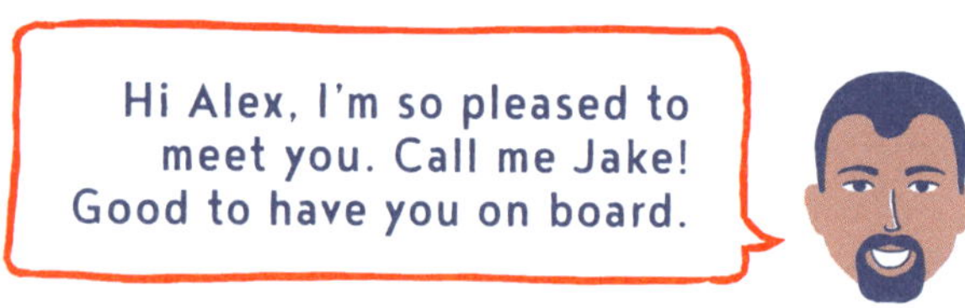

Lily's parents are more serious. Her Mom is tall and brown-haired. Her Dad's hair is turning grey. They are nice too, but not as cool as Diandra's parents. Lloyd Jessop, Lily's Dad, is a film director. He's directing Diandra's video clip. I'm impressed. I don't know how to talk to a film director!

SATURDAY 8TH JANUARY

La dame qui m'apporte mon petit déj'. s'est présentée. elle s'appelle Guadalupe.

So I phone Diandra from my luxury hotel room. Diandra says: SURE! Let's go!

* Museum of Modern Art

** Los Angeles County Museum of Art ou musée du comté de L.A.

Nous avons vu l'expo *Traverser les Frontières*, qui combine des poèmes de Blaise Cendrars (la prof de français serait contente) et le travail du plasticien Tony de Los Reyes.

VU AU LACMA
Tony de Los Reyes
Théorie de la Frontière

BORDER THEORY

GÉNIAL ! **WONDERFUL!** **AMAZING!**

C'étaient des photos aériennes du Rio Grande, le fleuve qui marque la frontière entre le Mexique (Mexico) et les USA. Super beau !

The US Mexican Border =
a living wound on the surface of America (Diandra said).

une plaie vivante

SUNDAY 9TH JANUARY

It's beautiful weather. It's sunny and warm!
I'm really happy!

PAS LE TEMPS D'ÉCRIRE !
NO TIME TO WRITE!

With Diandra's parents and her staff, we all spent the day on a yacht in a marina near L. A. We went swimming.

Prononcer : yotte

IT'S FANTASTIC IN L.A.

Dana West Marina

But the water is COLD! (Trop froide pour se baigner.)

TOMORROW, BACK TO SCHOOL!

MONDAY 10TH JANUARY!

It's great weather, it's sunny, but I'm so sad.

Après le week-end passé sur le yacht avec le staff et les parents de Diandra, je me faisais une joie de tout raconter à Lily ce matin, mais elle n'est pas en cours. J'ai demandé à tous les élèves de la classe :

RÉPONSES :

Harper

WHERE IS LILY?
Don't know. Maybe she's sick.

Guilia

WHY ISN'T LILY HERE?
No idea. Don't worry, she'll turn up.

Jose

DO YOU KNOW WHERE LILY IS?
Sorry, no. Haven't seen her since Friday.

At lunch, I tell Diandra Lily isn't here. Elle fronce les sourcils et envoie un SMS à Lloyd.

Lily absent. Where is she?

La réponse me fait froid dans le dos.

Lily missing since yesterday. Police here. Possibly kidnapped.

TUESDAY 11TH JANUARY

It's still beautiful weather, still sunny.

LILY IS STILL MISSING

This morning Harper sat next to me in school. Harper is nice, she's cool but she's a bit strange. I don't think Diandra likes Harper. Et vice versa.
Harper ne ressemble en rien à Lily et Diandra. Elle a des cheveux courts et des lunettes. Elle s'habille tout en noir, et elle dessine super bien.

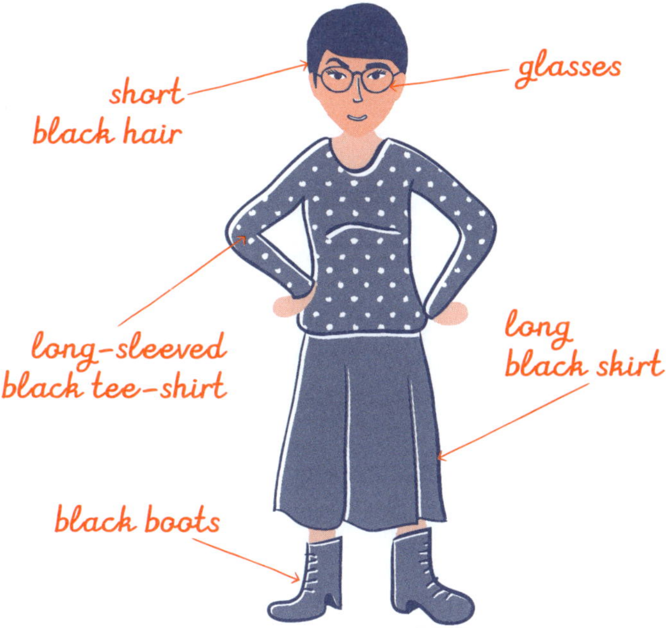

NOUS SOMMES EN COURS DE PHYSIQUE-CHIMIE

I hate physics and chemistry. Don't you hate physics and chemistry?

No, I say. I don't hate physics and chemistry. It's cool. I like science.

Harper me toise comme si j'étais le dernier des idiots.

Anyway, I've got something important to tell you. About Lily.

Quiet please ! Says the teacher. He isn't happy because Harper is talking. So she stops talking.

Je suis obligé d'attendre la pause pour écouter ce qu'elle veut me dire à propos de Lily ! L'attente est intenable !

WHAT HARPER SAYS:

**I like Lily. She's nice to me.
So listen, there's something strange about her disappearing from her house like that. There's no evidence of a kidnapping. No proof.
No clues. You understand?
Something's not right.**

Comment elle sait qu'il n'y a pas de preuves ou d'indices qui feraient penser à un kidnapping ?

WHAT I SAY:

How you know this?

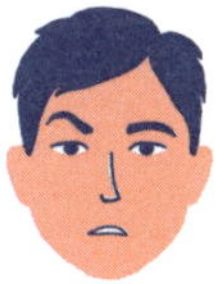

WHAT HARPER SAYS:

How do I know that? Because my dad is the Sheriff in charge of the inquiry. Now, are you listening or not?

(il me semblait bien qu'il y avait un « do » quelque part = I know, how do I know?)

*genre commissaire de police en charge de l'enquête.

J'écoute. I listen. Même si je pensais que les shérifs n'existaient que dans les westerns avec des cow-boys et des Indiens. Harper énumère sur ses doigts tous les indices qui laissent penser que Lily ne s'est pas fait enlever.

ONE: The Jessop's house has a security alarm that didn't go off.

TWO: No forced entry, broken windows, that sort of thing.

THREE: The dog didn't bark. Woof, woof, woof. No woof, woof.

So. What do you think?

**Me? Je n'en pense rien.
I don't know. No idea.**

Listen. I think Lloyd Jessop's murdered her and buried her body in the garden.

Il me faut une minute pour comprendre ce que Harper pense : Lloyd a tué Lily et enterré son corps dans le jardin.

WHAT???

Harper insists:

Lloyd Jessop is one strange guy.

Yes. But. I count on my fingers. Because...

ONE: The security alarm didn't go off,

TWO: There was no forced entry,

THREE: No woof woof,

... Harper thinks Lloyd Jessop killed Lily. But **WHY?** Why would Lloyd Jessop kill his daughter Lily? Apparemment Harper n'a pas été jusqu'à imaginer un mobile.

WHY???

Elle hausse les épaules.

I don't know. Because he's strange? He's a strange guy and strange guys do strange things, don't they?

Pas vraiment une raison pour tuer sa propre fille, non ?

LUNCH TIME

Chicken and salad

Je retrouve Diandra et lui raconte l'hypothèse de Harper dans laquelle le père de Lily tue sa fille et l'enterre dans le jardin parce qu'il est **STRANGE.**

It's Harper Diez who's strange.

You don't like Harper?

But Harper's dad is Sheriff.

Diandra fait une grimace qui n'en finit pas, et j'éclate de rire.

So what? My dad's an accountant, but I'm hopeless at math. I can't count. And anyway, Alex, you're here to help me, not to solve the Mystery of Disappearing Lily.

Je trouvais ça bizarre que Diandra ne soit pas plus inquiète. Je lui ai posé la question, car moi, j'étais super inquiet pour Lily : « Aren't you worried about Lily? » No answer... C'est quand même bizarre.

Diandra is not happy.

Son prof de chant a annulé la séance parce qu'il devait travailler avec Lloyd Jessop qui n'était pas joignable. Son prof de danse était absent pour la même raison.

SINGING TEACHER ABSENT + DANCING TEACHER ABSENT = DIANDRA NOT HAPPY

Diandra wanted to play tennis with me. Mais moi, je voulais retrouver Lily. J'ai proposé : « Maybe we can help Harper's dad to find Lily? » Du coup, Diandra a répondu un truc que je n'ai pas compris, et elle est partie sans même me dire au-revoir.

NO GOODBYE

Perhaps Diandra doesn't like Lily?
Or perhaps Diandra is angry because I'm worried about Lily?

IN MY LUXURY ROOM

Watching TV. Diandra m'a planté, alors je suis rentré dans ma super chambre de luxe et j'ai allumé la télé. Aux informations, ils parlaient de Lily.

Ils ont montré Lloyd Jessop et sa femme filmés à leur insu. Ils avaient l'air catastrophés. Ça m'a rendu encore plus triste. Voir ces reportages aux informations, ce n'est pas du tout pareil quand tu connais les personnes concernées. Là, tout de suite, mes parents me manquent.

WEDNESDAY 12TH JANUARY

The weather is sunny. But I'm cloudy. I'm worried about Lily.

Hier soir, je n'avais pas le moral et pas envie de manger non plus. Mais après une bonne nuit de sommeil, j'avais faim. J'ai dit à Guadalupe, la dame qui apporte le petit déjeuner tous les matins : « I'm hungry as a wolf! », traduction libre de « j'ai une faim de loup ». Elle a rigolé. She's really nice. Elle sourit tout le temps, et m'appelle par mon prénom...

How are you doing, Alex? Good day yesterday, Alex? You like L.A., Alex?

À force, j'ai trouvé le courage de lui demander :

Euh... Do you know Lily Jessop? She's disappeared.

Yeah! I saw her on TV. The police are asking if anybody's seen her. It's sad. Pretty girl like her!

IN ENGLISH

Harper sits with me.

Daddy doesn't think Lloyd Jessop is the murderer.

Diandra doesn't think so too.

Either. When it's a negative comparison, you have to say « either », not « too ». Do you like eggs? No I don't like eggs. I don't like eggs either. Or better: graveyards. Tombs. You know.

J'ai compris. Tombes. Cimetières. Pourquoi elle me parle de cimetières ?

HARPER'S ENGLISH GRAMMAR LESSON

POSITIVE →

I like graveyards.
Alex likes graveyards too.

NEGATIVE →

Lily doesn't like graveyards.
Diandra doesn't like graveyards either.

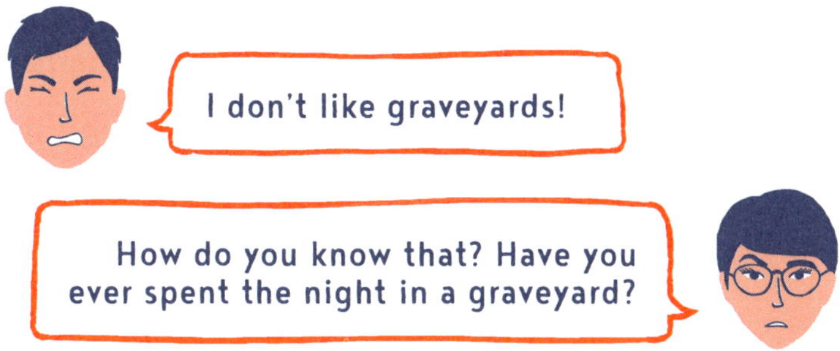

Est-ce que j'ai déjà passé une nuit dans un cimetière? Elle est folle ! Bien sûr que non.

Je ne sais pas pourquoi je sors cette phrase absurde..., Parce que au fond de moi je suis super triste et inquiet pour Lily qui est une fille super chouette, et je n'ai pas envie qu'il lui soit arrivé malheur. But Harper looks fascinated. Hey! That's a brilliant idea, she says. Je pense qu'elle n'a pas compris mon humour.

At lunch. Diandra looks better too. She ignores Harper.

– I'm sorry, she says to me. About yesterday.

– It's OK, I say. I'm sorry too.

– Listen, I was thinking, she goes on.

– Wow! That must have been a change for you, says Harper.

– What exactly is your problem? asks Diandra. Just because you're not sexy and talented, you don't have to hate the whole world.

– And just because you ARE sexy and talented, you don't have to hate people who aren't, says Harper.

I look at the ceiling. Nice ceiling.

Diandra et Harper se lancent des piques pendant cinq minutes. Je ne comprends pas tout.
I eat my hamburger and French fries still looking at the ceiling. Soudain, l'orage semble s'être calmé.

Oui, d'accord, peux mieux faire.

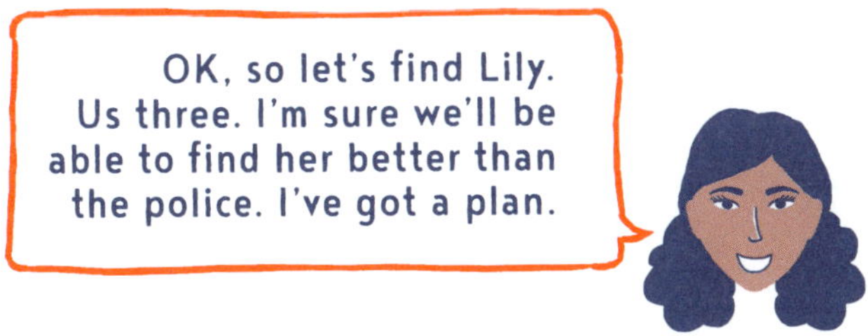

Harper agrees. We all agree. C'est mieux quand on est tous amis. En fait, je déteste les disputes.

DIANDRA'S PLAN IS SIMPLE:

HARPER MUST: Get as much information as possible about the police inquiry from her dad.

DIANDRA MUST: Get as much information as possible about Lily from Mr and Mrs Jessop.

I MUST: Get into the Jessop's house and search Lily's room.

WHAT???

Diandra explains:

Well, yes, Alex, I mean you can't really ask people questions, and anyway, you won't understand the answers, but you can use your eyes, can't you??

Et moi qui pensais avoir fait des progrès en anglais...

Harper et Diandra font la liste des endroits que je dois fouiller dans la chambre de Lily :

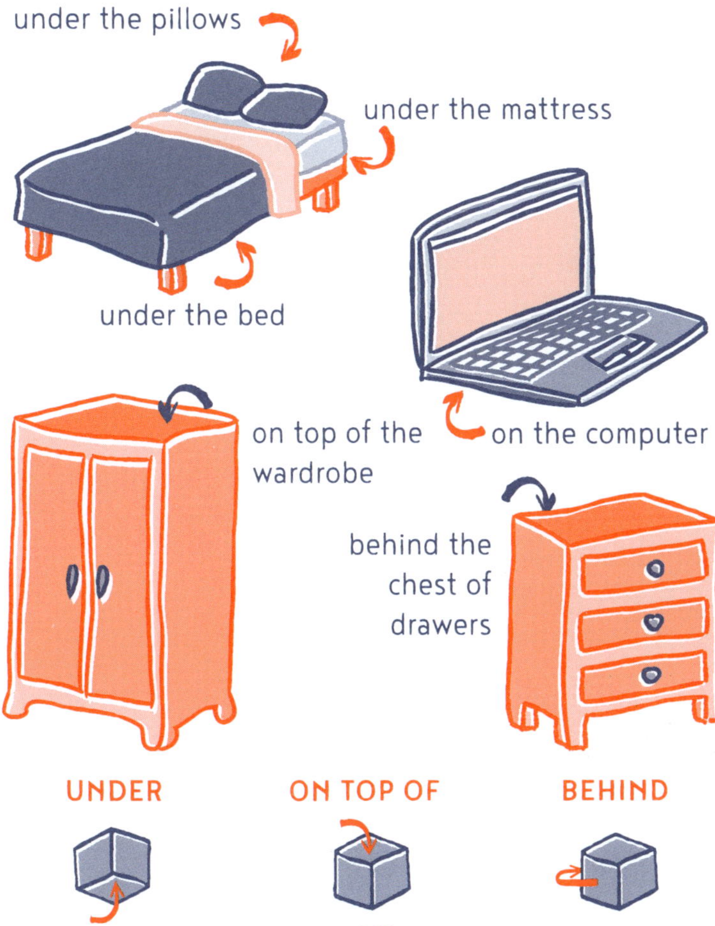

AND...
ANY POSSIBLE HIDING PLACE

WHAT'S A HIDING PLACE?

A place you hide something.

Harper

Diandra

A secret place no one can find.

Un endroit secret que personne ne peut trouver ? Je ne comprends rien, je commence à formuler une nouvelle question puis...

PING !
LUMIÈRE !
UNE CACHETTE !

Je dois trouver une cachette. Parfait.

Je ne vois qu'un obstacle à ma mission. Je mets du temps à me décider sur la formulation de ma question, puis je me lance :

Er... Guys... How do I get into Lily's room???

Diandra prend son téléphone portable, tape un message puis nous le montre.

Mom, I really need to see Lloyd Jessop. Can U ask if we can call round later? We want to ask about Lily. Say you've made a cake or something.

To call round = passer voir quelqu'un

Reply 2 mins later:

OK, we'll go and see them. But I don't have time 2 make a cake.

Diandra:

Well, buy one. We'll be back at 5.

NOTE:

WELL = «E» SHORT (tell, sell)

Le « e » court se prononce comme dans pelle

WE'LL = «E» LONG (wheel, seal, peel)

Le « e » long se prononce comme dans pile

IN MY LUXURY ROOM

Le prof de danse de Diandra (Dario) reprend les répétitions malgré l'absence de Lloyd Jessop. Mais il dit que j'empêche Diandra de travailler. C'est vrai que je lui fais des grimaces chaque fois qu'elle me regarde, et qu'elle éclate de rire. J'aurais mieux fait de m'abstenir parce que du coup :

Come on, Alex, you dance too!

Come on, Alex, jump!

Don't forget to breathe, Alex!

It's so hot here! Du coup, au bout de deux heures de danse, je suis épuisé, trempé, à court de souffle... I'm exhausted, drenched, breathless...

I NEED A SHOWER!!

The Jessops have invited us for drinks at six. J'ai juste le temps de me changer.

BACK FROM THE JESSOPS'

Lily's Mom's name is Caroline. Elle fait de son mieux pour nous accueillir, mais elle a l'air d'une zombie. Diandra lui pose des questions concernant Lily. Je ne comprends pas grand-chose. Comme convenu, au bout de quelques minutes, je murmure « bathroom » à l'oreille de Diandra qui dit :

On s'éloigne tous les deux vers un long couloir au sol de marbre.

J'ouvre la troisième porte sur la gauche.
It's like my luxury hotel room.

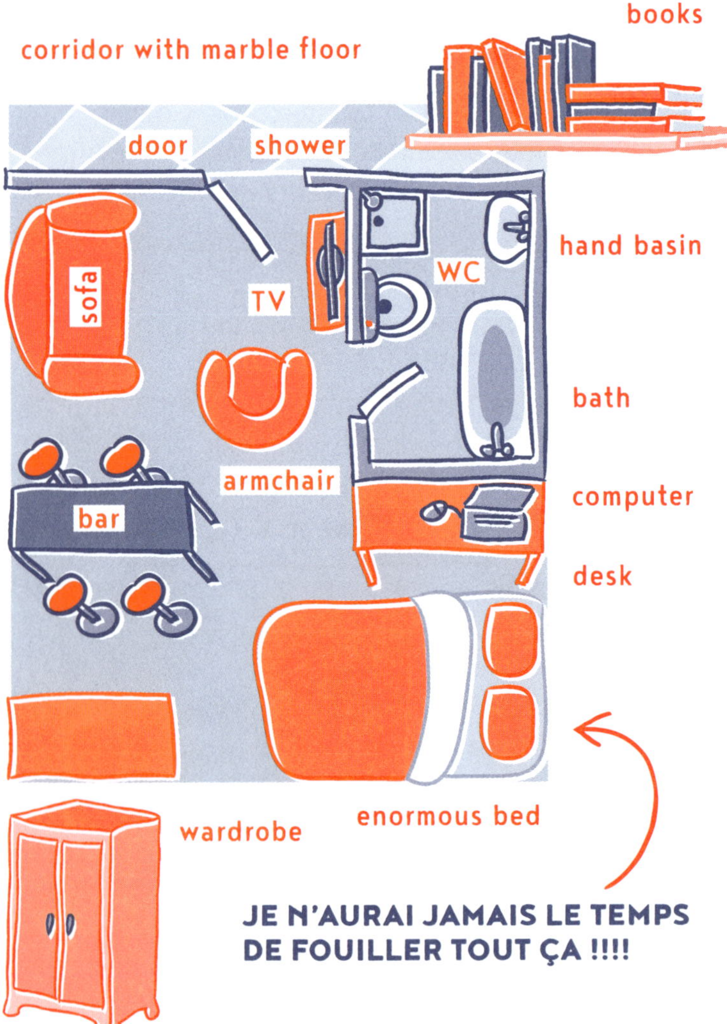

JE N'AURAI JAMAIS LE TEMPS DE FOUILLER TOUT ÇA !!!!

JE SUIS PRIS DE PANIQUE.

1. I don't have enough time.

2. This is Lily's room = It's intimate.

Je pense que Diandra et Harper n'ont pas bien réfléchi. Pour un garçon, fouiller une chambre de fille, c'est un peu gênant.

I'M A BOY ≠ SHE'S A GIRL

not the same!

SHE'S GOT GIRL THINGS IN HER ROOM.

I LOOKED

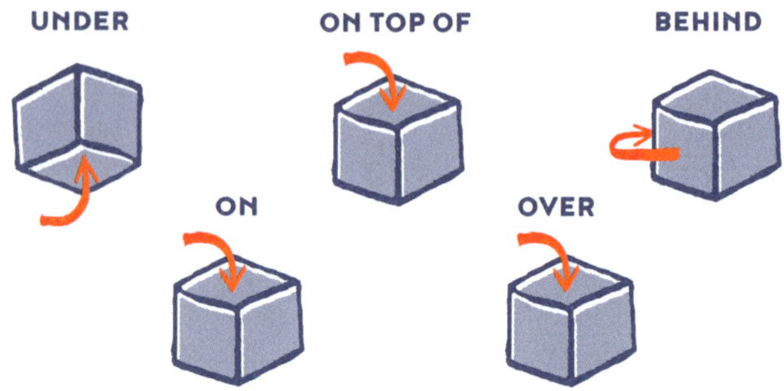

EVERYWHERE

I remember crime movies when the police or the hero searches a room. I flatten (je m'aplatis sur le ventre), then I crawl (like the cat in the poem) and I find...

NOTHING

TICK
TOCK
TICK
TOCK

I hear a clock ticking.

I don't have enough **TIME!**

Mon cœur bat tellement fort que si quelqu'un vient, je ne l'entendrai pas. Je m'efforce de respirer, comme pour la danse. I sit in Lily's armchair.

And suddenly, I see it.
Behind Lily's computer. A pink post-it...

This is what was stuck behind Lily's computer.

Strange.

What does it mean??

But no time to think.

Tout d'un coup, malgré mon cœur qui bat, j'entends des pas dans le couloir !

It's Caroline.

Alex? Are you OK?

PANIC!!

POST-IT → MY POCKET

ME → LILY'S BATHROOM

Je tire la chasse d'eau…

Alex? This is Lily's room, not the bathroom.

Oh! I'm so sorry. I opened doors, I saw a bathroom

(je dis ça en forçant à fond mon accent de Frenchie qui ne comprend rien)

Caroline a les larmes aux yeux en regardant la chambre de sa fille, et je m'en veux de lui mentir.

I'm sorry. I'm so sorry, I saw a bathroom…

THURSDAY 13TH JANUARY

The weather is perfect (not a surprise).
It's sunny (not a surprise).

In California, the weather is ALWAYS *perfect and sunny.* ← says Harper

But still no Lily. So everything is great and I'm sad.

This morning, we had a history lesson on...

THE WAR WITH MEXICO

1824 → Mexican independence from Spain
(before Mexico was a Spanish colony)

1836 → Texas Revolution → Texas becomes an independent State

1845 → Texas joins the USA → Mexicans not happy = WAR

1848 → Treaty of Guadalupe Hidalgo
(like the breakfast lady) = PEACE

Pendant que la guerre entre les États-Unis (le Texas) et le Mexique fait rage, je reprends avec Harper le sujet de ma découverte de la veille, en écrivant dans mon carnet de notes :

Yesterday, in Lily's bedroom, I found this post-it stuck behind Lily's computer.

On it, there was a list of names and question marks. Girls' names. Five names that seem Mexican.

Why did Lily hide five Mexican girls' names behind her computer?

NO IDEA

Harper wrote this.

LUNCH

Hot dogs. I love hot dogs.

Harper and I sit with Diandra in the canteen. Diandra searches again on her smartphone for Marisa Delgado. She says there are hundreds – thousands – millions of Marisa Delgados on the Internet...

AFTERNOON: DANCE

Dario said I must dance too. Again.

I HATE DANCING.

One, two, three, four...

I REALLY HATE DANCING...

AFTER DANCING, I NEED A...

SHOWER
AFTER SHOWERING
WE GO TO SHERIFF'S OFFICES

We meet Harper's dad. He's tall with blue eyes and a cowboy hat.

(It's like a police station = commissariat)

HARPER'S DAD
The Sheriff

This is a western! This is not real!

Harper

Harper's Dad

Harper: Hey Dad! Can we use your computer? It's for homework.

Harper's Dad: What's wrong with your computer at home?

Harper: It just died on me. PLEASE, Dad, this is URGENT. It's for TOMORROW!!

Harper's Dad: Harper... This is Sheriff Department stuff..

Harper: PLEASE!!
This is SCHOOL!!

Harper's Dad: Well... if it's for school... OK then...

Harper: THANK YOU!!
You're my favorite dad!!

Elle nous chuchote :

SCHOOL IS A MAGIC WORD...

Harper est impressionnante devant un ordinateur. Elle tape super vite, sans regarder les touches. Le logiciel demande un **PASSWORD** et immédiatement elle tape **HARPER**. Elle nous sourit. Le logiciel s'ouvre. Harper sélectionne **SEARCH ASSOCIATES** et entre les 5 noms écrits sur le post-it que j'ai trouvé derrière l'ordi de Lily.
Puis elle clique sur **SEARCH**.

(La recherche est lancée !)

THE SCREEN GOES BLANK

black screen = blank, nothing

I think this computer has just died too...
Then... Four words, one date :

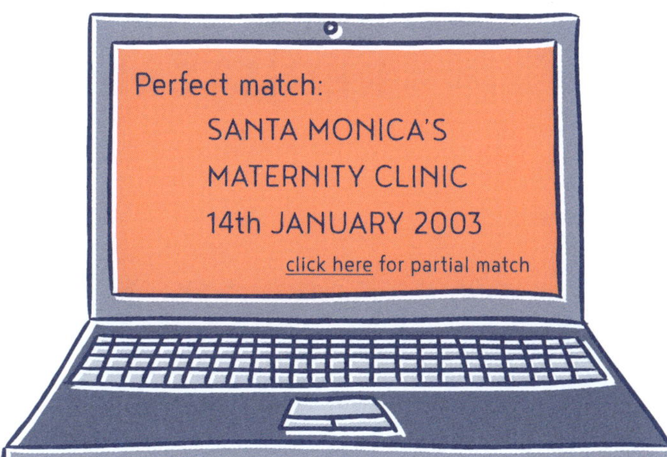

SANTA MONICA'S MATERNITY CLINIC 14TH JANUARY 2003

What's this???

What does it mean??

????????

I look at Harper. Harper looks at Diandra. Diandra looks at the computer, then at me...

??? ??? ??? ??? ??? ??? ??? ???

Harper opens an Internet search window and types in the place and the date.

The search engine shows 1 result:

BIRTHS REGISTERED

BIRTHS???

REGISTERED???

HEY!! says Harper suddenly.

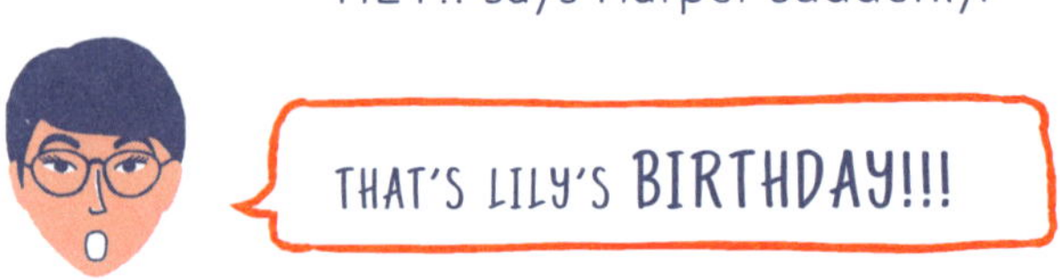

Harper tape le nom Lily Jessop dans le moteur de recherche de la clinique, et aussitôt s'affichent le nom de Lily et la même date, celle de son anniversaire. De toute évidence, Santa Monica's est une maternité, la clinique où Lily est née...
Mais c'est quoi, cette liste de noms ???

SANTA MONICA'S CLINIC
Surrogate Mothering Center

What's a Surrogate Mothering Center?

Harper and Diandra exchange looks. Harper turns red. Diandra hesitates, then asks me:

Alex, do you know how babies are made?

HA! HA!

Harper bursts out laughing. Diandra bursts out laughing. I turn red. VERY embarrassed with VERY red cheeks. Elles sont mortes de rire, du coup je ne sais plus quoi dire.

HA! HA!

This is soooo embarrassing.

No it's not. It's just biology.

Diandra takes a sheet of paper and this is her drawing:

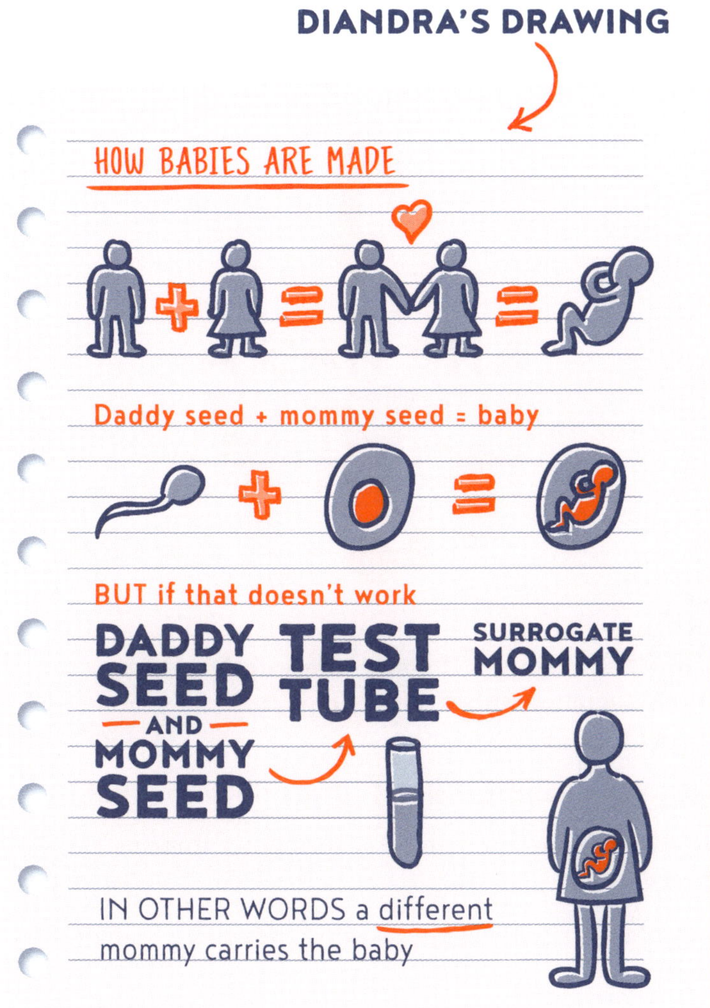

HARPER'S SUMMARY:

SO... Lily

MUST HAVE DISCOVERED

SHE HAS A SURROGATE MOTHER

qu'elle a une mère... porteuse ?

– But, says Harper, I'm not sure I understand (bienvenue au club). Caroline is still Lily's mom, right? Or not?

– Er, says Diandra. I'm not sure. I think so... But...

Je suis rassuré de constater que nous sommes trois à n'avoir pas compris.

– Biology teacher, says Diandra. We need some facts, here.

FRIDAY 14TH JANUARY

Sunny. Warm. Hollywood.
Today is Lily's birthday, but Lily's not here.
I'm really sad.

This morning we have biology.
Our biology teacher's name is Greg
(ici tout le monde s'appelle
par son prénom, y compris
les élèves et leurs profs).

Greg is tall and blond.
He's a surfer.

Harper asks:

Greg, can you explain what a surrogate mother is? Like exactly?

Heu... Sure, Harper. Look, it goes like this.

Et il a commencé à dessiner au tableau.

WHAT IS A SURROGATE MOTHER?

Greg's drawing:

MOTHER'S EGG + FATHER'S SPERM = IN VITRO FERTILISATION

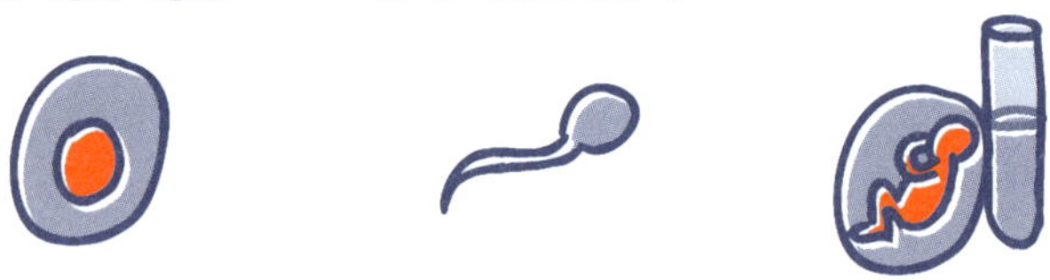

embryo implanted into surrogate mother's womb

GENETIC RELATIONSHIP TO BABY FROM BOTH PARENTS

(not from the pregnant woman)

Contract between genetic parents and surrogate mother (it's a paid contract in California).

Wow! You mean women actually get paid to have somebody else's baby?

Agitation générale !

Greg says: **QUIET PLEASE...**

QUIET PLEASE...

QUIET!!!

Le prof de bio est parti dans une longue explication concernant le corps, le travail et le système légal en Californie et ailleurs. Je n'ai pas tout compris (litote = quand tu dis un truc qui est bien en dessous de la vérité parce qu'en fait je n'ai rien compris) mais j'ai copié ceci du tableau =

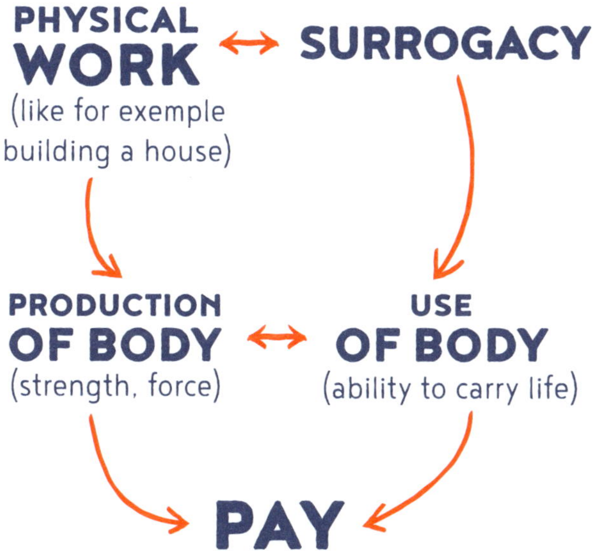

In California surrogate mothers are paid for the work of their body. Does carrying another couple's baby count as work?? Like a builder?? What about the USE of women's bodies, the psychological IMPACT on surrogate mothers and babies?

RÉSULTAT :

À la fin de la matinée, Harper et moi sommes imbattables (surtout Harper) sur la question des mères porteuses/de substitution/pour autrui ET sur la législation en Californie. Mais toujours dans le flou en ce qui concerne les conséquences psychologiques, l'exploitation du corps des femmes...

IT'S SO COMPLICATED.

But...

WHAT ABOUT LILY ??

LUNCH TIME

Fish fingers and chips (French fries).
It's always sunny (boring).

– Ok, says Diandra, eating her chips with her fingers. Where are we?

– We are that Lily was probably a test tube baby.

– Right. But what has that got to do with the fact that she's missing? Do you think her surrogate mother kidnapped her?

– No, said Harper. Women don't do that.

(je la trouve optimiste mais bon...)

The conversation between Harper and Diandra gives the following conclusions:

1. Lily must have discovered she has a surrogate mother. HOW??

2. Lily must have looked on the clinic website and made a list of the mothers who had babies on her birthday. (She must have known she was born at Santa Monica's).

3. Lily must have gone to find her surrogate mother.

So, if we want to find Lily, we have to discover which name belongs to her surrogate mother.

POSSIBILITIES:

MAYBE we SHOULD ask the Police?
MAYBE we SHOULD ask at the clinic?
PERHAPS we SHOULD ask the Jessops?

HOW DO WE FIND LILY?

OBSTACLES:

The Police PROBABLY won't tell us anything.
The clinic PROBABLY won't tell us anything.
The Jessops PROBABLY won't tell us anything.

DEAD END

SO WHAT DO WE DO?

NOBODY KNOWS

Et en attendant, I'm back with Diandra in rehearsals and...

I HATE DANCING.

I HATE DARIO.

I hate jumping and turning and bending and knees up and touching the floor... I'm tired and hot and sweating and... my muscles HURT! J'ai MAL aux muscles.

I WANT TO MURDER DIANDRA'S DANCING TEACHER.

AND

ONE, TWO THREE, FOUR

... BANG!

DARIO IS DEAD...

AFTER A SHOWER

Je me demande comment on peut retrouver Lily. Même sans la liste de noms collée derrière son ordinateur (et rien ne nous dit que la police ne l'a pas denichée), le shérif doit savoir que Lily est née d'une mère porteuse, alors si la police n'a pas réussi à savoir où elle est, je ne vois pas comment nous trois allons y arriver. Surtout si Lily n'a pas envie qu'on la retrouve, ce qui semble être le cas. J'ai tellement mal aux jambes que ça m'empêche de réfléchir. Soudain le téléphone sonne, c'est Diandra.

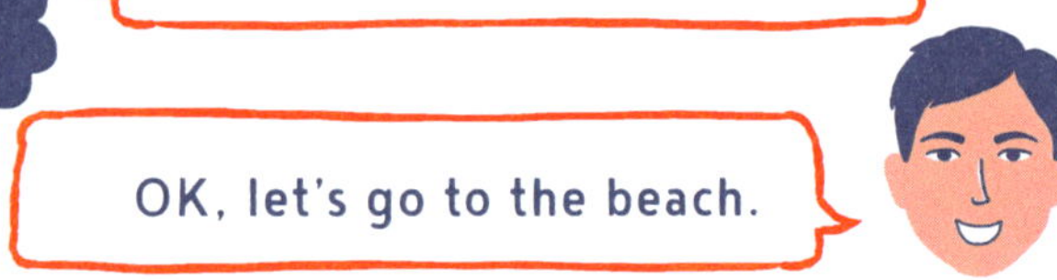

I walked on the beach with Diandra. As we walked, I asked questions.

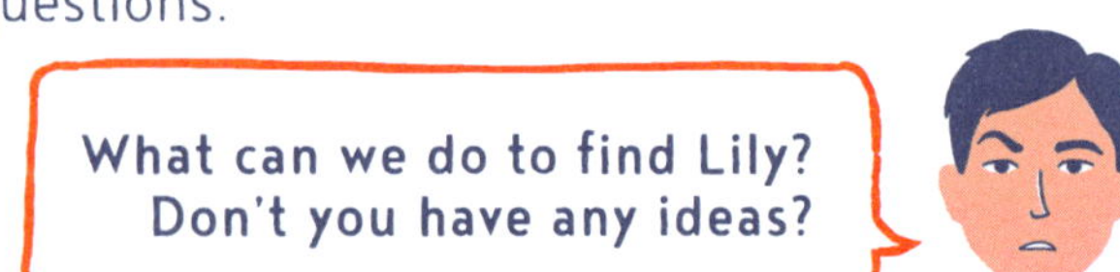

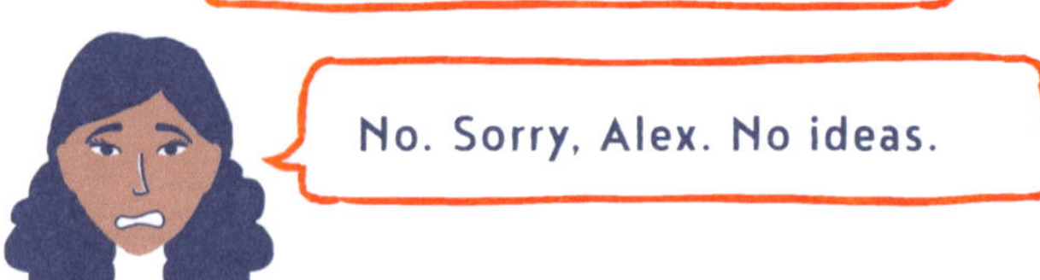

IN FRONT OF MY HOTEL

Harper is waiting!

Hey guys! At last you're here! Listen, we have to go and help the Sheriff's Department. Dad has made us all deputies*. Whe have to SAVE LILY.

Tout d'un coup, je pense au film *SAUVEZ WILLY* et j'ai envie de rire.

S'ensuit une conversation ultra rapide entre Lily et Harper. J'ai un peu l'impression d'écouter deux mitraillettes. Je comprends :

OK

RIGHT

SURROGATE MOM

MEXICAN BORDER

YEAH

* Deputies = des agents de police nommés par le shérif pour une raison précise et une durée déterminée.

Je suis devenu flic pendant 4 heures !

Puis Harper repart en courant vers une voiture du Sheriff's Department.

I ask Diandra.

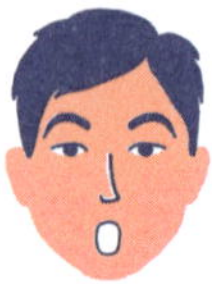

What's up?

They've found Lily down on the Mexican border with her surrogate mom. Her surrogate mom phoned the police. Lily is really sad, so the Sheriff wants us to talk to her, because we're her friends. We have to convince her to come home.

Je ne comprends pas trop. Pour moi, à 15 ans, on n'a pas vraiment le choix...

But she must come home.
She's 15! She has no choice!

Diandra smiles.

Yeah, well, legally, you're right, but... her parents want peace, not war.

Décidément, les Américains ne sont pas comme nous !

IN THE SHERIFF'S CAR

The Sheriff's deputy (adjoint) is driving us to the Mexican border to see Lily. The sheriff's car is BIG. J'en profite pour noter les mots que j'entends.

la route est large

The road is WIDE (not big, Diandra says. Big is a building, a road is flat and LONG or WIDE).

voyage et pas journée — *c'est loin*

The journey is LONG (it's a LONG WAY, Diandra says, 139 miles to the Mexican border, and since it's a long WAY it takes a long TIME because you can't drive FAST).

ça prend du temps — *on ne peut pas rouler vite*

aucune idée en kilomètres

We're driving DOWN ↓ to the Mexican border to TECATE (Tecate is on the border).

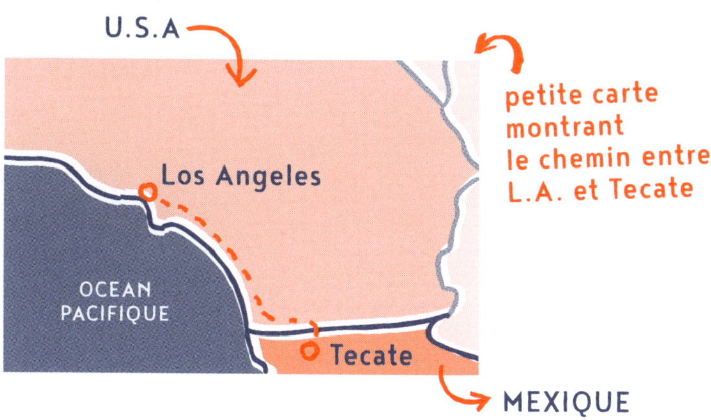

HARPER AND DIANDRA ARE TALKING ABOUT LILY.

TO BE ASHAMED = AVOIR HONTE

(Le père de Harper (The Sheriff) a regardé sur son smartphone. Il était super fier.

Je pense à Lily.
She's beautiful, she's intelligent, she lives in Hollywood, she's NICE, her dad's a film director... and she's ASHAMED??? I don't understand.
Harper explains:

This is Hollywood, right? Like I said, in Hollywood, we're all perfect. We have perfect teeth, perfect skin, perfect smiles, perfect homes, a perfect life. We're all like in the movies. OK?

Well... Having a surrogate Mexican mother is NOT perfect.

It's stupid, but that's the USA. We're racist here. We don't like Afro-Americans (sorry, Diandra). We don't like Mexicans. That's how we are.

Diandra was silent. She looked sad.

Since Diandra has stopped speaking, Harper tells me about where we're going.

Tecate is a Border Town. There's just the border, and the border is to stop Mexicans entering the wonderful world of the USA. Mexico is poor, the US is rich. Mexicans want to come to the US to get rich. But the US doesn't want lots of poor Mexicans coming over, so they make a border to keep them out.

I think about Guadalupe, the breakfast lady. Je la vois tous les jours. La semaine, le week-end, elle travaille tout le temps. Ça doit être pour ça, parce qu'elle est pauvre et qu'elle doit beaucoup travailler pour vivre dans une ville de riches.

When we arrive in Tecate, it's dark (it's night time).

The Sheriff's driver stops the car in front of a small house. Les portes sont en bois verni et fer forgé, une grille en fer forgé laisse apercevoir un petit jardin derrière. Le toit est en tuiles, les murs en brique. Ça me semble typiquement mexicain.

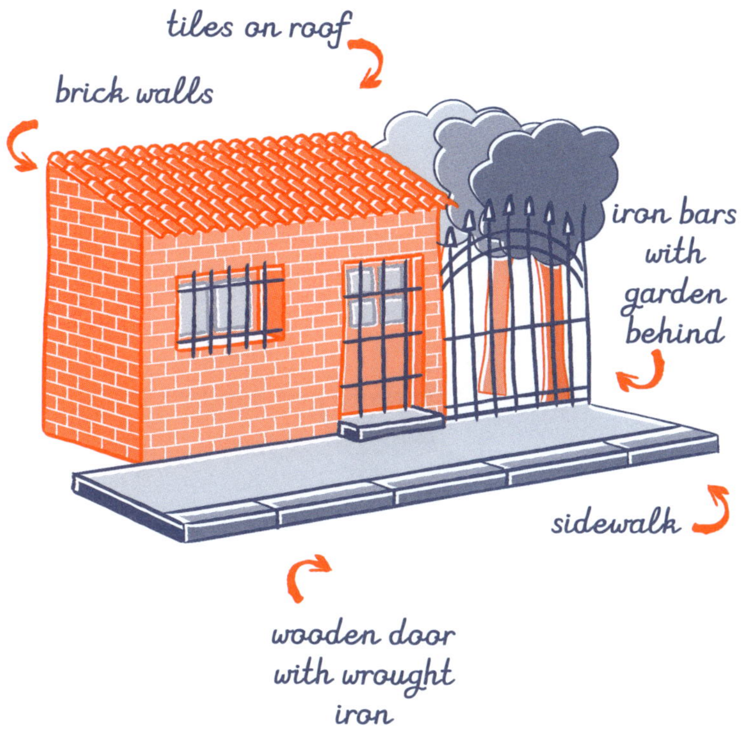

The Sheriff tells us to wait in the car.
Diandra is very quiet.
En fait, je me rends compte que D n'a rien dit depuis la remarque de H sur le racisme aux US.
J'essaie d'attirer le regard de mon amie, mais elle regarde par la fenêtre d'un air inquiet.
The Sheriff comes back.

Harper, Diandra et moi, nous nous lançons dans un brainstorming immédiat afin de trouver LA raison qui convaincra Lily de revenir chez ses parents plutôt que de rester chez sa mère porteuse mexicaine.

REASONS WHY LILY SHOULD COME BACK TO LA WITH US

1. Your Mom and Dad are sad.
2. Your Mom and Dad are your real parents.
3. You don't really know your surrogate mom.
4. Your dog misses you (→ that's my idea).
5. Your friends miss you (→ that's Harper's idea).
6. This is definitely not the best way to fight racism (→ that's Diandra's idea. I don't really understand).

WHEN WE'RE READY, WE SAY TO HARPER'S DAD:

OK! WE'RE READY!

When we get out of the car, it's night time but it's still really warm. The cicadas are singing.

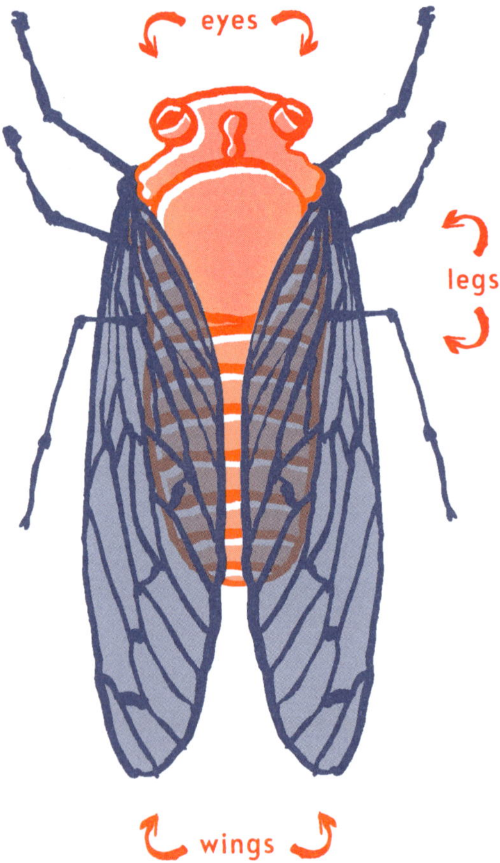

The cicada is a bug that makes a noise like a cricket.

CONSUELA

We go into the house. It's small and comfortable. It's very different from Lily's BIG house in Hollywood. A woman is in the kitchen.

She says:

Hi! You guys Lily's friends? You come all the way to Tecate to help her? That's cool. That's friends.

* Oui, Mrs Jones, je sais que ce n'est pas un anglais correct, mais l'anglais n'est pas la langue maternelle de Consuela.

In the living room, Lily is sitting on the sofa. She's not happy.

Lily, not looking at us:

Lily ne nous regarde pas. Elle parle d'une voix faussement heureuse.

Hi guys! Funny isn't it. Most people have only got one mother, but I've got two and neither of them really wants me... My mom in L.A. says I'm selfish* and Consuela says she's not my real mom, so here I am with nowhere to go...

*égoïste

On ouvre collectivement la bouche pour dire que ce n'est pas vrai, que ses deux mères l'aiment (je devine qu'elle a dû se disputer avec Caroline), mais Consuela est plus rapide que nous :

You know your problem, Lily Jessop? Your problem is you don't have no problem. You're rich, you're smart, you're cute, you're good at school, you have friends... hell, you're white! So you find the one thing that make* you different and you say THAT is a problem. Your parents gave me good money so you could exist. You should be ashamed of yourself!

On a tous regardé Consuela bouche bée. Moi, parce que je faisais de gros efforts pour comprendre, les filles parce qu'elles la trouvaient super dure... Elle a dû le sentir, parce qu'elle a ouvert les bras, et Lily s'est blottie contre elle.

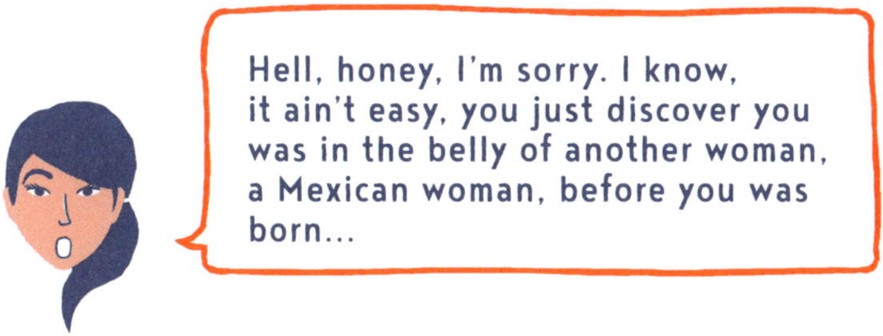

Lily s'essuie les yeux, se mouche, puis dit:

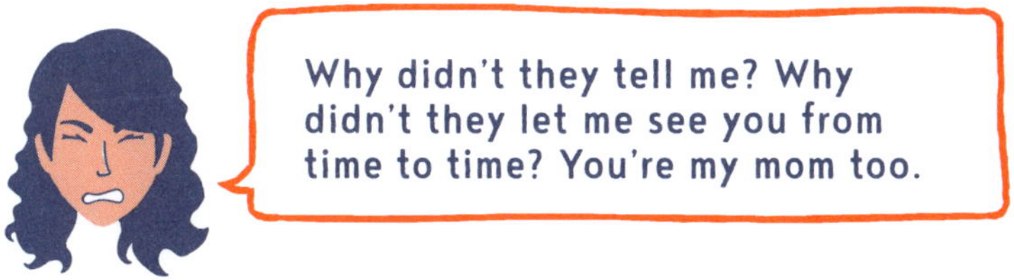

WHY? WHY?? WHY???

Consuela était visiblement dépassée par les événements.

Lily, honey, listen to me. Your parents are good people. They love you. They are there for you, they give you good house, good education, they want you to be happy. So OK, they don't tell you they can't have babies and they find this Mexican girl to have baby for them. OK. Maybe that's not so cool, but hell, that's ONE mistake. You gonna hate your parents for ONE mistake? Maybe they just wait for the good time and the good time don't come and they don't know how... But you gotta go back and talk to them. Running away ain't never the good solution.

J'étais d'accord avec Consuela. Oui, les parents de Lily auraient sans doute dû lui dire qu'ils avaient eu recours à une mère porteuse, mais s'enfuir n'était pas la meilleure façon de résoudre les problèmes.

Lily, said Consuela. I was happy to have you in my belly. Happy to give your parents a baby. Go back home, honey.

And then Lily smiled and it was OK. Lily said she would come back to L. A. So we all got into the Sheriff's BIG car. Consuela said she would come and visit Lily in L. A. Harper said she was hungry. The Sheriff said she would have to wait.

Lily

OK, I'll come back to L.A.

I'm HUNGRY

Harper

Sheriff

You'll have to wait

I'll come and visit you, Lily

Consuela

SATURDAY 15TH JANUARY

It was midnight when we got back to L.A. Lily said she didn't want to go back to her parents' house immediately. Diandra said she could come to our hotel. Harper said she wanted to come to our hotel too. Harper's dad the Sheriff said that was OK. He phoned Lily's parents and they said OK too. So we all went up to my luxury hotel room.

Harper wanted pizza, and Diandra said I should order the pizza because I had to practise speaking English. She gave me the phone. I must have made a strange face because she burst out laughing.

– Jesus!! Alex, you look like a fish on a bicycle!

= STUPID?

MA FIERTÉ A PRIS LE DESSUS. J'AI COMPOSÉ LE NUMÉRO.

ME ON THE PHONE

Me

Er... Hi! Can I order pizzas?

Well, that's what we're here for...

Pizza Man

Me

Sorry? Er...

What topping?

Harper

Burger topping double cheese.

I repeat on the phone.

Diandra

Pepperoni topping.

I repeat on the phone.

Lily

Tuna fish and mozarella.

I repeat on the phone and order pepperoni too.

Diandra, Harper and Lily LAUGHED for 10 minutes. Then Diandra called room service and ordered. 10 minutes later, the pizzas arrived. I had ordered a pepperoni. It was half past midnight. Diandra had ordered four bottles of diet soda. She took a bottle and held it up.

« HERE'S TO FRIENDS » A TOAST! HERE'S TO...

Then Diandra said:
Oh My GOD... Alex...

IT'S YOUR BIRTHDAY!

Diandra stood up and began to sing...

Happy birthday to you...

HARPER AND LILY JOINED IN.

Happy birthday to you...

IT WAS WONDERFUL.

Happy birthday to you...

Right, Alex.
What would you like for your birthday?

Nothing! I've got everything I want for my birthday. I'm in Hollywood, I'm in a luxury hotel, I'm with my best friend the rap star and two more wonderful friends. It's a perfect birthday. And I'm eating a real American pizza with diet soda. Thank you!

FAT TOMATO PIZZAS

1429 N Highland Av Los Angeles CA 90028

ANY PIZZA

Medium $22.43 | Large $25.43
Second pizza 50%

PEPPERONI
Red + yellow
pepper, sausage

CAPRESE
Tuna, mozzarella,
tomato, basil

BURGER
Beef, smoked
mozzarella,
red onion

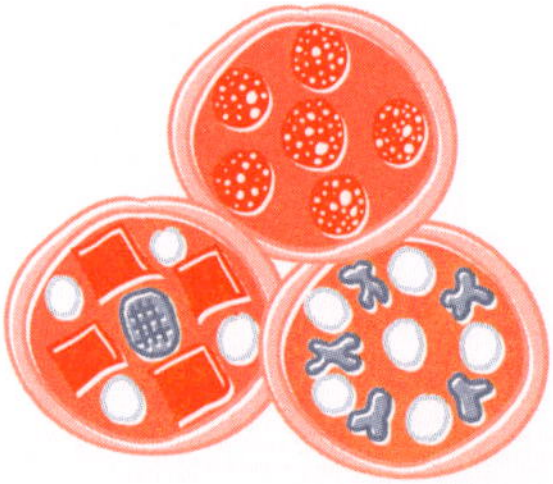

****

ROOM SERVICE
ROOM 604

4 large pizzas
2 PP
1 Caprese
1 Burger
4 diet cokes
1 tub ice-cream

****

MONDAY 17TH JANUARY

It's sunny and warm.

Lily is sitting next to me in math. I'm so happy.

Was it OK with your parents?

Yes, it was OK. I said I was sorry for leaving like that and making them worried. They said they were sorry they didn't tell me about Consuela and the whole surrogate mom thing. I said they should have told me years ago. They said I should have told them when I discovered the truth.

How did you discover the truth?

LILY'S STORY

It was a week or so ago. Just before you arrived, in fact. There was this girl I see when I have tennis lessons. I was talking about my birthday that was soon, and where I was born, and I said something about Santa Monica's fifteen years ago, and she said if I was born at Santa Monica's it meant I was born from a surrogate mom and that I was probably half Mexican, and she started making fun of me...

The math teacher tells us to stop talking.

I whisper:

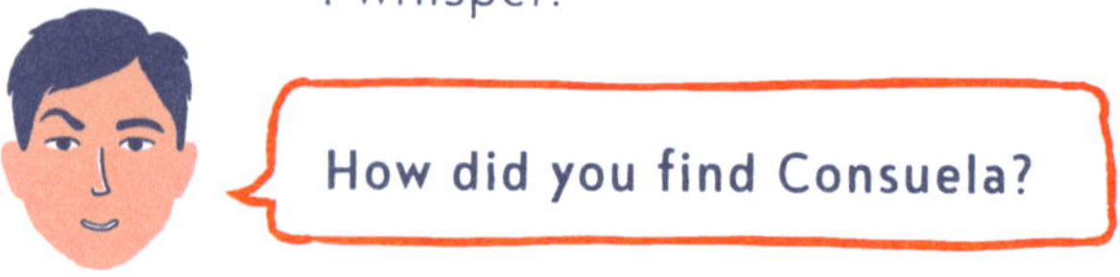

LILY WRITES ON HER COPY BOOK:

Page taken from Lily's math copy book

I went home and got out my birthday album, you know, those books where parents stick photos of their baby. At the back of my birthday book was a piece of paper with Santa Monica's letter heading and the date, the 14th January. There were 5 names of women who'd had babies on Jan. 14th, but no way of knowing which one was my surrogate mom. So I went into my dad's office at home and searched through all his stuff till I found one of the names, Consuela Amador. But I couldn't find an address or phone number. So I went out to Santa Monica's and pretended I knew I was born to a surrogate mom, like it was just normal. I asked if they had an address for my surrogate mom coz we'd lost it. And guess what? They gave it to me, just like that! EASY PEASY*!

* facile/fastoche

AFTERNOON

Lily and me with Diandra for her singing lesson.
Lloyd Jessop is here.
He really likes the way Diandra sings in French.
He says I'm a really good coach!

Lloyd Jessop

She sounds, you know, like so authentic... Well done, Alex, brilliant work!

AFTERNOON AGAIN

Lily and me with Diandra for her dancing lesson.
It's perfect.
I don't have to dance. I don't have to jump. I don't have to raise my arms. I don't have to turn. I don't have to put my knees up. I don't have to bend. I don't have to move up and down. I'm not hot. I'm not breathless. I just watch Diandra and the other dancers.
Easy peasy.
Lloyd Jessop is very happy.

TUESDAY 18TH JANUARY

Guess what?
The sun is shining!

In school this morning we had physics. We studied electricity. This is what Lily wrote in my physics book:

LUNCH

Fajitas and salad.

Sitting with Diandra, Harper and Lily.
Lily suggested we all go to the Fun Fair (fête foraine) in Anaheim (near Los Angeles) together on Saturday.

Reactions:

BRILLIANT IDEA!

GREAT!

AMAZING!!

YES!!

WONDERFUL!!

PERFECT!!

SENSATIONAL!

EXCELLENT!

SATURDAY 22ND JANUARY

Sunny weather, perfect day.

I'M EXHAUSTED!

We all went to the Fun Fair together. Lily and her parents, Diandra and her parents, Harper and her dad (her parents are separated), and me.
At the entry, Consuela was waiting for us. She had two balloons:

PICTURES OF THE FUN FAIR

Pirate boat

Horse race

Bumper cars

Big wheel

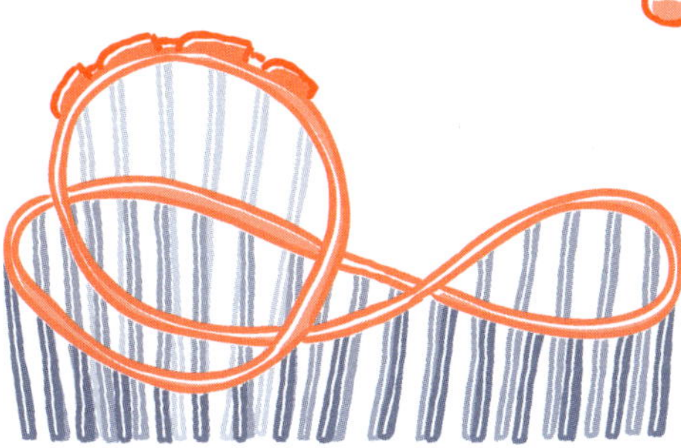

Rollercoaster

THURSDAY 27TH JANUARY

SORRY, I'VE BEEN NEGLECTING MY DIARY.

Diandra's new clip was released on MTV and YouTube. It was an immediate success. It had nearly 12 million views in just 6 hours!
Diandra is really happy, and Lloyd Jessop is happy too. And I'm really happy because Diandra's French pronunciation is PERFECT!
But I'm sad too because my winter in Hollywood is nearly finished.

THURSDAY 10TH FEBRUARY

ON THE PLANE BACK TO FRANCE.

MY BEST MEMORIES OF HOLLYWOOD:

1. Dancing with Diandra (because now it's finished).
2. Ordering pizzas on the phone (and watching the girls laugh for 10 minutes).
3. Visiting the LACMA (and the Border Theory photographs).
4. Finding the post-it stuck behind Lily's computer.
5. Saying to Lily: « I know in my heart we will see each other again. We're opposites who attract! »
6. Hearing Lily say: «Invite me to France. I know my dad will agree. I'll come and see you, I PROMISE.»

END OF HOLLYWOOD JOURNAL

L'AUTRICE

Stéphanie Benson est née à Londres en 1959. Arrivée en France en 1981, elle publie son premier roman pour adultes en 1995, puis se lance dans le roman policier jeunesse aux éditions Syros (*L'Inconnue dans la maison*, *La Disparue de la 6e B*, *Une Épine dans le pied*, *Shooting Star*...). Aujourd'hui autrice de plus de cinquante romans pour petits et grands (dont la série *Epicur* au Seuil), elle écrit également des nouvelles, de la poésie, ainsi que des pièces de théâtre dont des pièces radiophoniques pour France Inter et France Culture, et des scénarios pour la télévision. Parallèlement à sa vie d'autrice, elle est maître de conférences en anglais et didactique à l'université Bordeaux-Montaigne.

Crédits photos :

· Page 30 :

LOS ANGELES SEPTEMBER 2018: Los Angeles County Museum of Art, LACMA, in September 2018 in Los Angeles. It is located on Wilshire Blvd on Museum Row in the Mag Mile neighborhood.
© Shutterstock/ Pamela Brick

· Page 31 :

Dana Point, CA, USA March 24, 2008 The Orange County Harbor Patrol boat cruises through the marina in Dana Point, California.
© Shutterstock/ James Kirkikis

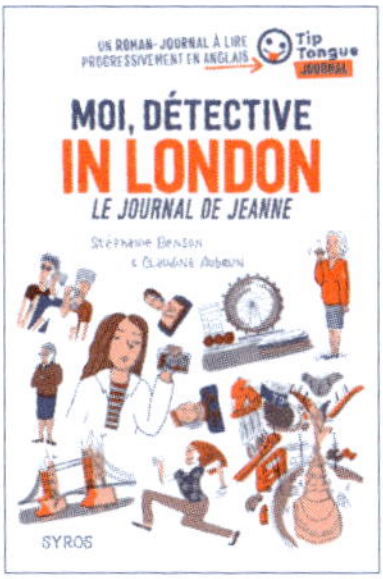

MOI, DÉTECTIVE IN LONDON

LE JOURNAL DE JEANNE

CLAUDINE AUBRUN ET STÉPHANIE BENSON

/ 8-10 ans /

Dès le CE2-CM1-CM2 / A1 INTRODUCTIF

80 p. (en 4 couleurs) / 12 x 18 / 6,95 €

Mots-clés : Amitié, Londres, écrivain, concert, enquête, polar

ISBN : 978274 8524802

MON AVENTURE IN GREEN

LE JOURNAL DE TOM

CLAUDINE AUBRUN ET STÉPHANIE BENSON

/ 10-12 ans /

Dès le CM2-6e-5e / A1 DÉCOUVERTE

96 p. (en 4 couleurs) / 12 x 18 / 6,95 €

Mots-clés : Amitié, correspondance, Écosse, écologie, enquête

ISBN : 978274 8524987

NOUVELLE STAR IN HOLLYWOOD

ALEX'S JOURNAL

STÉPHANIE BENSON

/ 12-14 ans /

Dès la 5e-4e-3e / A2 INTERMÉDIAIRE

112 p. (en 2 couleurs) / 12 x 18 / 6,95 €

Mots-clés : Amitié, musique, star, origines, Hollywood, Mexique

ISBN : 978274 8524949

LOVE ? IN NEW-YORK

CALLIE'S JOURNAL

STÉPHANIE BENSON

/ 14-16 ans /

Dès la 3e-2nde-1re / B1 SEUIL

112 p. (en 2 couleurs) / 12 x 18 / 6,95 €

Mots-clés : École d'art, New York, amour, inégalités

ISBN : 978274 8524703

Achevé d'imprimer en janvier 2019
par Pollina (85400 Luçon, France) - 87360

MIXTE
Papier issu de
sources responsables
FSC® C022030